Józef Korneliusz Trzebuniak SVD

Athenagoras
and
the Divine Logos

Legatio pro Christianis
De resurrectione mortuorum

Table of Contents

Introduction

The first Christian authors after the New Testament were the Apostolic Fathers, who, as disciples of the Apostles, passed on the Gospel in their writings.[1] These earliest writers of the Church were not a homogeneous group, but preachers from various philosophical backgrounds. They did not seek a scientific justification for Christianity or the truths of faith.[2] In their writings they did not directly raise issues connected to the concept of the divine Logos.[3] The texts of the Apostolic Fathers instead had a pastoral character and were concerned mainly with the problems of their contemporary Christian communities. They used the vocabulary of everyday life and there is thus no complex doctrinal content or profound philosophical speculation in their writings.

---

[1] This group includes seven writers: the author of the *Didache*, Clement of Rome, Ignatius, Polycarp, Hermas, Barnabas and Papias. The writings of the Apostolic Fathers have a pastoral character, they resemble apostolic letters in content and form, and they link the New Testament with the later Tradition.

[2] See B. Altaner, A. Stuiber, *Patrologia* [Patrology], Warszawa 1990, 105.

[3] The exception is St. Ignatius of Antioch, who claimed that Christ is a timeless, eternal and true God. Christ has the characteristics of the Logos, or the Incarnate Word of God, who has always existed in the Father. The Bishop of Antioch expressed his theology in a mystical language, and, like the Apostle John, encouraged all to keep unity with Christ. See Ignatius Antiochenus, *Ad Ephesios* 3.2-3; *Ad Romanos* 8.2; *Ad Magnesios* 1.2; 6.1; 7.1; 8.2. Ignatius called Christ "the thought of the Father" and "the lips that do not know the lies through which the Father truly spoke".

It was only in the second century that the Christian apologists began the so-called Christology of the Logos, which referred to both Greek and Jewish philosophy, as well as to biblical thought,[4] in presenting Christianity in a scientific and philosophically coherent way. In their speeches and writings, they defended the orthodoxy of the Christian faith and presented the very teaching of the Church.[5] These apologists generally accepted that the Old Testament has a doctrinal authority and is part of the Christian inheritance. In their deliberations they took up anthropological issues and accepted a dichotomous division of human nature. They based their philosophical arguments on the teachings of the New Testament, which they knew from both the apostolic letters and the Gospel, as well as from liturgical practices and the catechetical tradition of the Church.[6] In so doing, they treated the entire content of the Holy Scriptures as one.[7]

---

[4] See L. Zygner, "Formuła «światłość ze światłości» w okresie przednicejskim" [*"Light from Light" formula of the Ante-Nicene period*], *Vox Patrum* 13-15 (1993) 324.

[5] See H. Pietras, *Początki teologii Kościoła* [The Beginnings of Church Theology], Kraków 2007, 38–39.

[6] See M. Fiedrowicz, *Teologia Ojców Kościoła* [Theology of Fathers of the Church], Kraków 2009, 56-59.

[7] See J.N.D. Kelly, *Początki doktryny chrześcijańskiej* [Early Christian

This book presents the teaching of Athenagoras as it relates to the concept of participation in the Divine Logos. The theology of apologists was the theology of educated people who had lost confidence in the polytheistic religions and Hellenic philosophy. However, the apologists did not entirely reject the heritage of ancient culture. While they sought to translate the Christian faith into philosophical and theological language by employing the conceptual apparatus of their own era, they nevertheless also used the terminology of the philosophers of ancient times, especially that of the Stoics and Middle Platonists.

In their arguments, usually in the form of speeches, treatises or dialogues,[8] the apologists thus used concepts from classical philosophy that were familiar to their adversaries.[9] They began by presenting Christianity as a philosophy, much like Philo of Alexandria, who pinpointed the close relationship between revealed

---

Doctrines], Warszawa 1988, 36.

[8] The apologists used various literary genres that were common in Hellenic literature, while their choice of arguments and literary composition depended on the specific audience to whom their writings were addressed. See A. Żurek, *Ojcowie Kościoła – twórcy i świadkowie Tradycji* [Fathers of the Church - Creators and Witnesses of Tradition], Tarnów 2013, 53-56.

[9] See M. Wysocki, *Argumenty wczesnochrześcijańskich apologetów za wyższością chrześcijaństwa nad innymi religiami* [Arguments of the Early Christian Apologists for the Superiority of Christianity over Other Religions], in: I. S. Ledwoń, M. Szram, *Wczesne chrześcijaństwo a religie* [Early Christianity and Religions], Lublin 2012, 133-134.

religion and Greek philosophy. Moreover, they drew inspiration from the Prologue to the Gospel of John, in which the author identifies Christ as the eternal Logos and Son of God. In this way, using the concept of the Logos, they translated Christianity into a language that was understood in the culture of the Greco-Roman world.[10]

At the time of the second-century Christian apologists, the study of the Logos was booming, and the catechumens saw in Christianity the ultimate fulfilment of ancient philosophy. These apologists were thus the precursors of those who would later intellectually explain the relationship between creation and the Creator,[11] the relationship of Christ to God the Father, and the Logos in men, angels and the whole world created by God.[12]

---

[10]See P. Hadot, *Czym jest filozofia starożytna?* [What is Ancient Philosophy], Warszawa 2000, 297-299.

[11]See R.M. Leszczyński, *Starożytna koncepcja Logosu* [The Ancient Concept of the Logos], Warszawa 2003, 211-214.

[12] See J.N.D. Kelly, *Początki doktryny chrześcijańskiej* [Early Christian Doctrines], Warszawa 1998, 80.

The Life of Athenagoras

Athenagoras, an Athenian philosopher and convert to Christianity, was one of the most outstanding and interesting apologists of the second century.[13]After his conversion, he became an ardent defender of the Christian faith. He was writing in the times of Emperors Marcus Aurelius and Commodus, to whom he addressed his memorial in defence of Christians.[14] Of his writings only two genuine pieces have been preserved: his apology, *The Request for Christians* addressed to the Emperor, which was written in 177, and a *Treatise on the Resurrection* of 36 chapters.[15] His works take a special place among apologists because of their content and the quality of their style.

The Athenian philosopher was the first to explain the Christian truth about the resurrection of the

---

[13] See L.R. Lanzillotta, *Christian Apologists and Greek Gods*, in: J.N. Bremmer, and A. Erskine (eds.), *The Gods of Ancient Greece* (Edinburgh, 2010), 457-460.

[14] An English translation is found in *Ante-Nicene Fathers,* Vol. 2: *Fathers of the Second Century: Hermes, Tatian, Athenagoras, Theophilus, and Clement of Alexandria (Entire)*, ed. Alexander Roberts and James Donaldson. Revised and chronologically arranged with brief prefaces and occasional notes by A. Cleveland Coxe (New York 1903).

[15] The Greek text of the writings of Athenagoras according to the edition of *Patrologia graeca.*The best editions of *Legatio pro Christianis* and *De resurrectione mortuorum* are those of Otto, *Corpus Apologetarum* (Jena, 1857), VII, and the Benedictine Maranus in *Patrologia graeca* (Paris, 1857), VI, 889-1024.

body. When writing about the mystery of the Holy Trinity and the Son of God, he used classical concepts of the Greek language, such asvoῦςand λόγος. He also described the presence of God in the Christian community and pointed to the positive influence of the Christian religion on morality.[16] He was always tolerant of pagan views, valued Greek philosophy highly, and respected his emperors. Aware that Marcus Aurelius was a Stoic, he drew many arguments from Stoic philosophy.

On some issues Athenagoras points to the correspondence between the wisdom of the ancient philosophers and the Christian teachings, and also between state and Church. He affirms the truths of the faith with philosophical arguments in order to defend Christians in times of persecution. Knowing that his readers do not know the truths of Christianity, he convinces them that faith does not have to oppose reason. He argues that true Christian philosophy places the whole person at the centre of its deliberations, not just the soul.[17] In his apologies, Athenagoras

---

[16] See J.M. Szymusiak, M. Starowieyski, *Słownik wczesnochrześcijańskiego piśmiennictwa*[Dictionary of Early Christian Literature], Poznań 1971, 60.

[17]See E. Gilson, *Historia filozofii chrześcijańskiej w wiekach średnich*

demonstrates a philosophical way of thinking, and shares his reflections in the context of the writings of Greek philosophers and poets.

[History of Christian Philosophy in the Middle Ages], Warszawa 1921, 19-21.

Legatio pro Christianis

The apology *Request for Christians* appears to be a public speech addressed to Emperor Marcus Aurelius and his son Commodus. In it, the apologist states that the persecution of Christians is based on a slander. To refute the allegations against Christianity, Athenagoras presents the basic principles of the religion and criticizes pagan theology. He argues that Christians are not atheists and that their teaching agrees with the monotheism of ancient philosophers such as Pythagoras, Plato and the Stoics. He nevertheless emphasizes the superiority of Christian doctrine, which comes from the supreme God, and describes it as follows:

> *Our doctrine acknowledges one God,*
> *the Maker of this universe, who is*
> *Himself uncreated (for that which is*
> *does not come to be, but that which is*
> *not) but has made all things by the*
> *Logos which is from Him.*[18]

The Athenian draws inspiration for his deliberations on the Logos, Son of God, mainly from the *Prologue* of John's Gospel.[19]Furthermore, he claims that the Scriptures contain the truths revealed by God himself, and are in line with the teaching of ancient philosophers. According to Athenagoras, the divine Logos can only be understood through the understanding and reason (νῷ μόνῳ καὶ λόγῳ):

> *He is the first product of the Father, not*
> *as having been brought into existence*
> *(for from the beginning, God, who is the*
> *eternal mind [νοῦς], had the Logos in*
> *Himself, being from eternity instinct*
> *with Logos [λογικός]); but inasmuch as*
> *He came forth to be the idea and*

---

[18] Athenagoras, *Legatio pro Christianis* 4 (PG 6, 283C).
[19] See Jn. 1:3.14.

energizing power of all material things.[20]

Christians have the privilege of knowing the Son of God, who is the Word of God. They know that this truth should not be understood in the same way as the myths told by the poets. Instead, they seek to understand it in the spirit of the Gospel, although using terms derived from Greek philosophers. In his apology, Athenagoras presents this argument as follows:

> *The Son of God is the Logos of the Father, in idea and in operation; for after the pattern of Him and by Him were all things made, the Father and the Son being one. And, the Son being in the Father and the Father in the Son, in oneness and power of spirit, the understanding and reason (νοῦς καὶ λόγος) of the Father is the Son of God.*[21]

---

[20] Athenagoras, *Legatio pro Christianis* 10 (PG 6, 286B).
[21] Athenagoras, *Legatio pro Christianis* 10 (PG 6, 286B). See also Jn. 1:3; 10:38; Col. 1:16-20.

This passage highlights the rational aspect of the Logos-Son, who manifests the divine intelligence and the creative power of God the Father.[22] Describing the operation of the Logos, the apologist points to the Platonic idea (ἰδέα) and Aristotelian energy (ἐνεργεία).[23] In Athenagoras' theology, the Son of God is the model upon whom humans are created and also the acting power that creates them. This teaching coincides with the words of the prophets, who expressed the same thought in different words.[24] Furthermore, the Logos reveals his action in the world and in humans through other spiritual beings:

> *God the Maker and Framer of the world distributed and appointed to their several posts by His Logos, to occupy themselves about the elements, and the heavens, and the world, and the things in it, and the goodly ordering of them all.*[25]

---

[22] See L. W. Barnard, *Athenagoras: A Study in Second Century Christian Apologetic* (Paris 1972), 97.

[23] Athenagoras refers not only to the philosophy of Plato and Aristotle, but also to Philo of Alexandria. In his apology, the Logos is a Platonic-Philonian idea and the model of all material beings. The Logos is the exemplary cause of the created world and the efficient cause of the creation. Moreover, the Logos does not exist outside God, but within God.

[24] See Prov. 8:22.

[25] Athenagoras, *Legatio pro Christianis* 10 (PG 6, 286B).

The Logos is not merely the expression of God's action and the manifestation of the divine Person. Following the gospel doctrine, the whole universe is destined for the Logos, who deals with it also after the act of creation. Through divine providence, the Logos guards all beings in wisdom and justice.[26]Accordingly, Christians choose a life that is moderate, benevolent, modest and peaceful.[27] Athenagoras identifies himself with such and explains further in *The Request for Christians*:

> *While men who reckon the present life of very small worth indeed, and who are conducted to the future life by this one thing alone, that they know God and His Logos, what is the oneness of the Son with the Father, what the communion of the Father with the Son, what is the Spirit, what is the unity of these three, the Spirit, the Son, the Father, and their distinction in unity.*[28]

---

[26] See Athenagoras, *De resurrectione mortuorum* 18.

[27] Athenagoras, *Legatio pro Christianis* 12, S. Kalinkowski, p. 41. See also Rom. 8:18.

[28] Athenagoras, *Legatio pro Christianis* 12 (PG 6, 289C).

Thus, the aim of the Christian life is to fully understand the unity found in God. Christians correctly believe in one God and his Logos who orders the universe. Consequently, they better comprehend the conviction of the Stoics that it is the Logos who creates harmony in the created world. The laws of nature give proof of the existence of the divine Logos and the observation of the cosmos leads to true devotion. The essence of piety is to realize that the Logos continuously looks after the world and maintains the existence of all creatures.[29]

Humans are part of creation and therefore should worship their Creator, who is inaccessible Light, perfect World, Spirit, Power and Reason (λόγος). According to Athenagoras, the world is God's beautiful art (τέχνη τοῦ Θεοῦ), and believers are to respect the Artist for his perfect composition. Following the Peripatetic doctrine, Athenagoras agrees that the world is a substance and body. Consequently, human beings are to worship the only God who is the cause of the movements of this body.[30]

---

[29] See R.M. Leszczyński, *Starożytna koncepcja Logosu* [The Ancient Concept of Logos], Warszawa 2003, 253.
[30] See Athenagoras, *Legatio pro Christianis* 16.

Athenagoras then chooses a Stoic way of proving the existence of God, a proof based also on the beauty of creation and the purposefulness in the universe. He uses teleological evidence and presents a hierarchical arrangement of beings. In his opinion, God the Father supervises everything with the help of his Son-Logos. Thus the Creator assigns individual spheres of the cosmos to angels and permeates individual beings through his Spirit. Athenagoras describes this process in the next passage of his apology:

> *For, as we acknowledge a God, and a Son his Logos, and a Holy Spirit, united in essence-the Father, the Son, the Spirit, because the Son is the Intelligence, Reason, Wisdom of the Father, and the Spirit an effluence, as light from fire; so also do we apprehend the existence of other powers, which exercise dominion about matter.*[31]

The author of *Request for Christians* points to an ontological difference between the self-existing God, his

---

[31] Athenagoras, *Legatio pro Christianis* 24 (PG 6, 302B).

Logos and the created world, which does not possess full existence. According to this fundamental order, all created beings are subject to constant passing, and also to the eternal and uncreated Logos who is the principle of their existence.[32] The creatures that are particularly subject to God's protection are human beings. The apologist writes:

> *Of those things which belong to the constitution of the whole world there is nothing out of order or neglected, but that each one of them has been produced by reason, and that, therefore, they do not transgress the order prescribed to them.*[33]

However, people can surrender to the action of evil spirits that have influence both on individuals and on entire nations, internally and externally. Such people are unable to perceive the order in the universe and tend to argue that everything has an irrational cause. Against this, Athenagoras argues that every element of the world is created according to reason and cannot exceed the order that has been assigned to it. This divine order

---

[32] See R.M. Leszczyński, *Starożytna koncepcja Logosu*, Warszawa 2003, 254.
[33] Athenagoras, *Legatio pro Christianis* 25 (PG 6, 304C).

applies to all people, who have been given the ability of reason (λογισμόν), even though they often make mistakes because of the operation of malevolent demons. This is described in detail in the apology, as follows:

> *Man himself, too, so far as He that made him is concerned, is well ordered, both by his original nature, which has one common character for all, and by the constitution of his body, which does not transgress the law imposed upon it, and by the termination of his life, which remains equal and common to all alike; but that, according to the character peculiar to himself and the operation of the ruling prince and of the demons his followers, he is impelled and moved in this direction or in that, notwithstanding that all possess in common the same original constitution of mind.*[34]

Athenagoras believes it is matter that has transformed itself into the kingdom of evil and is used by the demons use to deceive people. At the beginning of

---

[34] Athenagoras, *Legatio pro Christianis* 25 (PG 6, 304C).

creation, the good angels ruled parts of the world according to the laws of the Logos, but the angel who ruled matter departed from God and was joined by other evil angels.[35] These angels are now followed by people whose souls are drawn to matter. They no longer look for heavenly things and their Creator, but descend to earthly things and thus become a part of the material world, which is flesh and blood, and not pure spirit.[36]

The Christian apologist emphasizes that God should be the basic standard of conduct for humanity. Only if this happens people can live impeccably. Christians endeavour to dwell on the earth in this way and thus take part in the order of the divine Logos, until eventually they become united with God in heaven. This idea is reflected in the following:

> *We know that God is witness to what we think and what we say both by night and by day, and that He, being Himself light, sees all things in our heart. We are persuaded that when we are removed from the present life we shall live another life, better than the present*

---

[35]See S. Świeżawski, *Dzieje europejskiej filozofii klasycznej* [The History of European Classical Philosophy], Warszawa-Wrocław 2000, 276.
[36]See Athenagoras, *Legatio pro Christianis* 27.

one, and heavenly, not earthly (since we shall abide near God, and with God, free from all change or suffering in the soul, not as flesh, even though we shall have flesh, but as heavenly spirit).[37]

Unfortunately, there are those who, instead of striving for a more perfect union with God and the Logos, choose the opposite direction and as a result will live in the midst of fire. This applies to those who have deliberately committed sins and offered themselves for the punishment of the Great Judge. It was obviously not the intention of the Creator that people perish or be annihilated; hence, God sends his Logos with a new commandment of love and the norm of justice.[38]

Athenagoras concludes his apology by expressing strong hope for eternal life and the desire to be united with God. He explains that many Christians choose virginity and celibacy in order to consecrate themselves to God. They strictly obey the commandments contained in the New Testament. Furthermore, they prefer to be servants, not masters of

---

[37]Athenagoras, *Legatio pro Christianis* 31 (PG 6, 309C). See also 1 Jn. 1:5.
[38] See Mt. 22:37-40; Mk. 12:28-31; Lk. 10:25-28; Jn. 13:34-35.

reason.[39] They embrace the truth that God-Logos accepted the human body to fulfil the divine plan and save humankind.[40]

According to the teaching of Athenagoras, the participation of the world in the Logos confirms that all created beings are constantly subject to divine providence. Further, the Athenian philosopher emphasizes the ontological participation of the entire universe in the Divine Logos. Following the example of Christians, all people should strive to understand and acknowledge the cosmic order that the Logos instilled in the world. Participation in the Incarnate Logos also means knowing God through faith and keeping his commandments. Athenagoras was the first Christian author to suggest that an ascetic life of celibacy and virginity can lead to a deeper participation in the Logos.

---

[39] See Athenagoras, *Legatio pro Christianis* 35.
[40] See Athenagoras, *Legatio pro Christianis* 21.

De resurrectione mortuorum

The second apology of Athenagoras is crucial in the history of Christian anthropology. The purpose is to defend one specific truth of the Christian faith that pagans could not accept. The apologist justifies faith in the resurrection on the basis of reason and also biblical teaching.[41] He explains the possibility of the resurrection is based on God's omnipotence. In addition, he writes about the rationality, justice and the aspiration of human beings to everlasting happiness, and asserts that every person is an entity composed of soul and body:

---

[41] See A. Żurek, *Ojcowie Kościoła–twórcy i świadkowie Tradycji* [Fathers of the Church: Creators and Witnesses of Tradition], Tarnów 2013, 60-61.

> *The whole nature of men in general is composed of an immortal soul and a body which was fitted to it in the creation.*[42]

The human person, as a complex being of soul and body, is endowed with understanding and reason (νοῦν καὶ λόγον) and is destined for permanent existence. The union of the soul with the body is most beneficial for humans and subsequently demands permanence.[43] In his apologetic treatise, Athenagoras makes the following argument:

> *Man, therefore, who consists of the two parts, must continue forever. But it is impossible for him to continue unless he rise again. For if no resurrection were to take place, the nature of men as men would not continue.*[44]

All human actions require sensual and mental evaluation, according to Athenagoras. Thus, a human being strives for eternal life, and everything is structured

---

[42] Athenagoras, *De resurrectione mortuorum* 15 (PG 6, 328A).
[43] S. Świeżawski, *Dzieje europejskiej filozofii klasycznej* [History of European Classical Philosophy], Warszawa -Wrocław 2000, 276-277.
[44] Athenagoras, *De resurrectione mortuorum* 15 (PG 6, 328D).

into a harmonious arrangement, namely his origin, nature, existence, deeds, life and purpose. This happens in accordance with God's plan, which was established before centuries and testifies to the dignity and wisdom of God who knows the nature of humans and their destination.[45]

Athenagoras also describes the divine power (δύναμις) through which the Creator forms the world and sustains it in existence. He states that the Creator of the world has sufficient power to cause the resurrection of bodies.[46]Because he always acts according to reason, he created human beings as entities endowed with understanding and a rational judgment. In the *Treatise on the Resurrection* Athenagoras describes the fundamental cause of creation as follows:

> *The cause itself is bound up with its nature, and is recognised only in connection with existence itself, can never admit of any cause which shall utterly annihilate its existence. But since this cause is seen to lie in perpetual*

---

[45] See Athenagoras, *De resurrectione mortuorum* 2.
[46] See Athenagoras, *De resurrectione mortuorum*3.

existence, the being so created must be preserved for ever.[47]

Accordingly, the two most important reasons for the creation of human beings are firstly, the wisdom and goodness of God, which is manifested in his works, and secondly, the eternal existence of human beings who, thanks to the image of the Creator, take part in the Logos and rational judgement. The Creator gives them these gifts so they can know the divine power and wisdom. Through obedience to the law and justice, they are able to exist eternally and full of virtue.[48] They should acquire virtue in the present life, so that after death they can experience the resurrection of their body:

> *The Maker of this universe made man with a view to his partaking of an intelligent life, and that, having become a spectator of His grandeur, and of the wisdom which is manifest in all things, he might continue always in the contemplation of these; then, according*

---

[47] Athenagoras, *De resurrectione mortuorum* 12 (PG 6, 325B).
[48] See E. Gilson, *Historia filozofii chrześcijańskiej w wiekach średnich* [History of Christian Philosophy in the Middle Ages], Warszawa 1921, 20.

*to the purpose of his Author, and the
nature which he has received.*[49]

The purpose behind creation should encourage everyone to strive for eternal participation in the Divine Logos. This can only happen if the two parts of man have the same destiny, indicating a harmony between soul and body. Since the purpose of both parts are identical to that of the whole, the ultimate purpose is the resurrection of the human person.

In his apology, Athenagoras explains that partaking in the resurrection only concerns human beings. It happens in accordance with God's will and justice. The apologist indicates different degrees of participation in the divine Logos, clearly stating that God does not give the same end to beings who are not of identical nature.[50]

On earth, people reside in mortal and suffering bodies, but after death they will live in immortal bodies that will no longer experience suffering. This is the plan and will of God, who in his wisdom is capable of making

---

[49] Athenagoras, *De resurrectione mortuorum* 13 (PG 6, 326C).
[50] See Athenagoras, *De resurrectione mortuorum* 10.

things even more perfect and of creating bodies that are immortal and not subject to suffering. In addition, Athenagoras gives a reason why eternity only concerns human beings:

> *For whatever has been created for the sake of something else, when that has ceased to be for the sake of which it was created, will itself also fitly cease to be, and will not continue to exist in vain, since, among the works of God, that which is useless can have no place; but that which was created for the very purpose of existing and living a life naturally suited to it, since the cause itself is bound up with its nature, and is recognised only in connection with existence itself, can never admit of any cause which shall utterly annihilate its existence.*[51]

Therefore, people should retain a strong hope for permanent existence in the Divine Logos. According to God's plan, the human being is made of an immortal soul and body (ἐκ ψυχῆς ἀθανάτου καὶ σόματος) and is endowed with reason and inborn law (νοῦν καὶ νόμον

---

[51] Athenagoras, *De resurrectione mortuorum* 12 (PG 6, 325C).

ἔμφυτον). During this earthly journey, he should try to respect God's gifts, which are compatible with a reasonable life (ζωῇ λογικῇ), so that in eternal life, after undergoing judgment, he may receive a just reward and experience the joy of seeing God.[52] The apologist summarizes in these words:

> *The final cause of an intelligent life and rational judgment, is to be occupied uninterruptedly with those objects to which the natural reason is chiefly and primarily adapted, and to delight unceasingly in the contemplation of Him who is, and of His decrees.*[53]

The writings of Athenagoras reveal that the philosopher was more interested in the cosmic Logos, which was the main topic of his contemporaries, than in the historical figure of Jesus Christ from the Scriptures and the works of the Apostolic Fathers. The aim of his apologies was to convince the Greeks and Romans of the truth of Christianity by using rational arguments from

---

[52] See Athenagoras, *De resurrectione mortuorum* 25.
[53] Athenagoras, *De resurrectione mortuorum* 24 (PG 6, 335D). See also 1 Cor. 15:53; 2 Cor. 5:10.

their own religious-philosophical background. Identifying the divine Logos with the cosmic principle of the universe, Athenagoras revealed Christianity as a universal and rational religion.[54]

---

[54] See R.M. Leszczyński, *Starożytna koncepcja Logosu i jej wpływ na myśl wczesnego chrześcijaństwa* [The Ancient Concept of the Logos], Warszawa 2003, 255.

Conclusion

In his apologies *Legatio pro Christianis* and *De resurrectione mortuorum*, Athenagoras draws abundantly both from the thoughts of the Greek philosophers - Plato, Aristotle, the Stoics - as well as from the reflections of Philo of Alexandria, John the Evangelist and Apostle Paul. God creates, orders and maintains everything through his Logos. The Logos of God is described as the Platonic idea (ἰδέα) by which people are formed, and also the Aristotelian energy (ἐνεργεία), namely, the working power that creates humanity for eternal participation in God's happiness. The Athenian Philosopher confirms that the Logos manifests his presence in the world through spiritual beings. Ultimately, the main task of all human beings is to partake in the order given by the divine Logos[55].

---

[55] The book is based on a PhD dissertation that was originally published in the Polish language: J. Trzebuniak, "Uczestnictwo w boskim Logosie według greckich Ojców Kościoła II wieku" [Participation in the Divine Logos according to the Greek Fathers of the Church of the Second Century], Verbinum (2019), 1-245.

References

Ante-Nicene Fathers. Volume 2: Fathers of the Second Century: Hermes, Tatian, Athenagoras, Theophilus, and Clement of Alexandria (Entire),ed. Alexander Roberts and James Donaldson. Revised and chronologically arranged with brief prefaces and occasional notes by A. Cleveland Coxe (New York 1903).

Athenagoras, *Legatio pro Christianis*, Patrologia graeca (Paris, 1857), VI.

Athenagoras, *De resurrectione mortuorum*, Patrologia graeca (Paris, 1857), VI.

Barnard L. W., *Athenagoras. A Study in Second Century Christian Apologetic* (Paris 1972).

Bober, A., *Antologia patrystyczna* [*Patristic Anthology*], Kraków 1965.

Chadwick, H., *Myśl wczesnochrześcijańska a tradycja klasyczna* [*Early Christian Thought and Classical Tradition*], Poznań 2000.

Cullan, J., *The Seeds of Dialogue in Justin Martyr*, Australian eJournal of Theology 7.6 (2006).

Daniélou, J., *Gospel Message and Hellenistic Culture* (London, 1973).

Fiedrowicz, M., Teologia Ojców Kościoła [*Theology of Fathers of the Church*], Kraków 2009.

Gilson, E., *Historia filozofii chrześcijańskiej w wiekach średnich* [History of Christian Philosophy in the Middle Ages], Warszawa 1921.

Hadot, P., *Czym jest filozofia starożytna?*[*What is Ancient Philosophy*], Warszawa 2000.

Kelly, J.N.D., *Początki doktryny chrześcijańskiej* [*Early Christian Doctrines*], Warszawa 1998.

Leszczyński, R.M., *Starożytna koncepcja Logosu* [*The Ancient Concept of Logos*], Warszawa 2003.

Lanzillotta, L.R.,*Christian Apologists and Greek Gods*, in: J.N. Bremmer, A. Erskine (ed.), *The Gods of Ancient Greece* (Edinburgh 2010), 457-460.

Mrugalski, D., *Logos. Filozoficzne i teologiczne źródła idei wczesnochrześcijańskiej* [*Philosophical and theological sources of early Christian ideas*], Kraków 2006.

Nestle, E. (ed.), *Novum Testamentum Graece et Latine* (Stuttgart 1921).

Pietras, H., *Początki teologii Kościoła* [*The Beginnings of Church Theology*], Kraków 2007.

Świeżawski, S., *Dzieje europejskiej filozofii klasycznej* [*History of European Classical Philosophy*], Warszawa–Wrocław 2000.

Szymusiak, J.M. Starowieyski, M., *Słownik wczesnochrześcijańskiego piśmiennictwa*, [*Dictionary of Early Christian Literature*], Poznań 1971.

Trzebuniak, J., "*Uczestnictwo w boskim Logosie według greckich Ojców Kościoła II wieku*" [*"Participation in the Divine Logos according to the Greek Fathers of the Church of the Second Century"*], Verbinum (2019).

Zygner, L., "*Formuła «światłość ze światłości» w okresie przednicejskim*" [*"Light from Light" formula of the Ante-Nicene period*], Vox Patrum 13-15 (1993).

Żurek, A., *Ojcowie Kościoła – twórcy i świadkowie Tradycji* [*Fathers of the Church - Creators and Witnesses of Tradition*], Tarnów 2013.

9 798681 558545